THE CONTENT OF
INDIAN AND IRANIAN
STUDIES

T0346171

THE CONTENT OF
INDIAN & IRANIAN
STUDIES

AN INAUGURAL LECTURE DELIVERED
ON 2 MAY 1938

by

H. W. BAILEY

*Fellow of Queens' College and Professor
of Sanskrit in the University
of Cambridge*

CAMBRIDGE

AT THE UNIVERSITY PRESS

1938

CAMBRIDGE
UNIVERSITY PRESS

University Printing House, Cambridge CB2 8BS, United Kingdom

Published in the United States of America by Cambridge University Press, New York

Cambridge University Press is part of the University of Cambridge.

It furthers the University's mission by disseminating knowledge in the pursuit of
education, learning and research at the highest international levels of excellence.

www.cambridge.org
Information on this title: www.cambridge.org/9781107634176

© Cambridge University Press 1938

First published 1938
Re-issued 2014

A catalogue record for this publication is available from the British Library

ISBN 9781107634176 Paperback

THE CONTENT OF INDIAN AND IRANIAN STUDIES

Sanskrit as the title of a University Chair has something of simplicity to recommend it. But simplicity may be deceptive, and if we should insist upon interpreting rigorously the word Sanskrit in this title, that is, in the sense of the Indian word *saṃskṛta*, the learned language of India as regulated and refined by the grammarians, we should reach the paradoxical position that more than half of our present Sanskrit syllabus would be excluded. It was my purpose in proposing to give this lecture to indicate in the manner of a modest programme what is embraced in this wider study. For the same reason I have entitled this lecture not 'The Content of Sanskrit Studies', but 'The Content of Indian and Iranian Studies'. It is the study of a culture which has become two but was originally one, and of which

(5)

the later developments came once again into close contact.

I may speak first of Indian studies. It is interesting to see how the countries to the west of India have come to a knowledge of things Indian. Within India itself Sanskrit and its allied literatures, though in the north checked to some extent by the Muhammadan incursions, were maintained without break from the earliest records. Outside India we see in the west that the Persians early interested themselves in this literature. Two famous collections of stories, the book of beast fables, the Sanskrit Pancatantra, which was known in a Persian translation in Persia in the sixth century under the Sasanian kings, and the book of the legend of the Bodhisattva, that is, the aspirant to Buddhist enlightenment, under the name of Barlaam and Joasaph, spread through Persia and Syria to the whole Islamic world and to other parts of Europe. One great student we know, the Muhammadan scholar, the Chorasmian Al-Bairūnī, who lived from A.D. 973 to 1048. He stands out from his fellows. To secure solid results for his book on India, he made himself familiar with Sanskrit, then, as for many now, the language of learning in India. But there were among the Arabs and Persians no studies, no editions and no encyclopaedias gathering up Sanskrit learning in the original language. In Europe exact knowledge of Sanskrit came as something of a revelation in the eighteenth century. From that time its influence has spread till little in the humanities has been left unaffected. But at first books were hard to procure, and some reluctance had to be overcome, a reluctance, easily understood, to initiate foreigners into a sacred tradition. With this western knowledge we shall contrast the countries to the east of India. There during the early Christian centuries, Chinese and other scholars were assiduously and enthusiastically reading and translating Sanskrit.

It is pleasantly refreshing to observe the first contact of Europeans under the influence of their tradition of classical scholarship with this new matter of research. There was a keen appreciation of the literary treasures, as the enthusiastic welcome of Kālidāsa's drama *Śakuntalā* shows. The linguistic importance of the Sanskrit language was at once recognized. We observe how eagerly the scanty available texts were read, how for the first time the methods of classical research were applied to an Indian language. Editions of short texts were made, the story of Nala and Damayantī, and of Arjuna's journey to heaven. The philosophical didactic poem called the Bhagavadgītā was among the earlier publications. These texts were not in the oldest form of the Indian language, but they served nevertheless to point the way to the beginnings of comparative grammar. In this the elaborate analysis carried out centuries earlier by the Indian grammarians proved of great assistance. Meantime with a great enthusiasm the search for the oldest Indian literature was carried on. By 1863 Aufrecht had brought out the first complete edition of the Rigveda, the oldest and linguistically the most important text.

I need not delay long to-day over the content of Sanskrit literature. It will be familiar to all in the many histories of Sanskrit literature, which have been published in the past hundred years, in English, French, German and other languages. But I should here perhaps indicate briefly the course of this literary development. The oldest texts are the poetical Vedas, books held in particular honour, and the ancillary literature containing explanations of the ritual, philosophical speculations and legends. The four chief collections were named from the use to which their verses were put, the Rigveda, the book of hymns, the Yajurveda, the book of sacrificial formulae, the Sāmaveda, the book of chantings, and the Atharvaveda, the book of magical spells. The dates of these books unhappily for us did not interest the composers or the collectors or those who transmitted them. But the oldest parts are hardly likely to be later than about 1200 B.C. As to the contents, some of the poems of the Rigveda, which are wholly religious in character, read with remarkable freshness. That they should have been quoted later in books of rather wearisome theology is the fate of many a book deemed sacred. The collection of the Atharvaveda is full of the formulae of magic, of blessings and curses, and magical promises. It touches a side of life almost entirely different from the Rigveda. After the Vedas came the explanations, the Brāhmaṇas. But it requires an extraordinarily sympathetic mind to enjoy their contents. In striking contrast stand the philosophical treatises known under the name of Upaniṣads, which have been widely read and enjoyed. Law books follow, based on religious doctrines, then the political and ethical manuals. The grammarians stand apart. The grammars are treatises of high precision. One especial grammar, that of Pāṇini, whom an Indian tradition places in the fourth century B.C., cannot be passed over unnamed. It offers us an invaluable record of the language which was recognized to be standard in the north-west of India in his time. He was, however, not blind to other standards, as he shows by quoting at times, for our taste all too rarely, divergences of the language of the East. Epic poetry is represented for us in two great poems, the Mahābhārata, a huge disparate collection, repository of numerous legends and didactic admonitions, and the Rāmāyaṇa, simpler, less interpolated, the gracious story of Rāma and his stolen wife, a story beloved in India as in the lands which received Indian culture. Long eulogies of kings, the praśasti as they are called, are carved on the rocks, for the inscriptions of India are legion. Drama, lyrical and gnomic poetry flourished wonderfully. And I ought perhaps not to forget completely the modern use of Sanskrit. One reads, in a recent History of Sanskrit Literature from South India, for example, that the English paraphrase of the Persian Omar Khayyam, which we owe to Fitzgerald, has been rendered into Sanskrit which is 'superb'. In South India particularly, there has been very considerable activity in Sanskrit composition to the present day.

This Vedic and Sanskrit literature is vast enough in itself. But it is no longer possible to be content with Indian literature in these two forms of the Old Indian language. It has now long been recognized that without some knowledge of the later forms of the language, which we conveniently associate under the name Middle Indian (or Middle Indo-Aryan, to distinguish it from other non-Aryan languages of India), and the literatures preserved in them, only a distorted view of Indian culture and history can result. This later development of the Old Indian language is known to us in many different forms. Originally, and largely at all times, these distinctions were due to divergent provincial changes. The dialects can be particularly clearly traced in the earliest inscriptions, those of Aśoka in the third century B.C. The north-western, the western and the eastern dialects are easily recognized. Fragments of dramas have been found using this early type of Middle Indian, but it is in a slightly later form that we know most of the dialects, at a time when they were largely used in dramatic compositions, chiefly for inferior characters and women, sometimes indeed exclusively. Two large collections of Middle Indian texts owe their origin to the foundation of particular religions, those of the Jainas and the Buddhists. The older Jaina literature is preserved in two dialects, which we call Ardha-Māgadhī and Māhārāṣṭrī. The Buddhists used a variety of Middle Indian dialects. The most complete collection has reached us in a form of Western Indian and is now widely known under the name of Pali. Inscriptions are likewise found in a variety of dialects from the time of Aśoka onwards.

It will not be possible here to speak of the recent developments in the New Indian languages such as Sinhalese, Gujarati, Hindi, Panjabi, Marathi and Bengali. For linguistic study these languages are of great importance. Each too has developed its own literature, and one poem, the story of Rāma, in the Rāma-carita-mānasa of Tulasī-dāsa in the Awadhī language has had a great fortune. There are bright prospects for the future of these languages.

I should here intercalate a few words on the scripts used in recording this enormous literary output. One script, the recently discovered writing of the Indus Valley, does not concern us here. It is not used for the literature I have mentioned. But two other scripts have been in use. They have been designated by names from the Sanskrit books as the Kharoṣṭhī and the Brāhmī. The origin of the Kharoṣṭhī is known. It is a variety of the Aramaic alphabet of Syria. It was a script of North-western India and was carried thence to the Indian settlements of Central Asia beyond Khotan. It is known to us chiefly from documents and inscriptions, but a literature did at one time exist in it of which fragments have survived. The second script, the Brāhmī, whose origin is to some minds still un-decided, is the script of all India in a great variety of modifications. It spread with Indian culture to the south-eastern lands as far as Cambodia.

It has a home in the decorative script of Java. It went to Tibet, to Bactria and eastwards to Kashghar, Khotan, Kuci, Agni and the Turks. The Chinese Buddhists used it in China, and to the present day the script has been handed down in Buddhist connections in Japan. The variety of form is great but the system is one. For the expression of Indian sounds it has been phonetically excellent. For other peoples it required considerable modification and at least twenty-two new signs were ultimately invented in Central Asia. The Khotanese were satisfied to give new values to existing signs, producing thereby a somewhat cumbrous system, and the Turks tried both methods to increase its usefulness. Other scripts, such as the Arabic modification of the Aramaic script, which have been used in India need not detain us here.

I must now turn to consider Iranian studies. By the Iranian or Eranian, for the English spelling and pronunciation of the word is still unfixed, we refer to a group of languages and to a large literature, which belong to Persia and the lands adjacent to Persia to the north and east, to the regions beyond Khotan. Persian itself is one member of this group. How indispensable Iranian studies are for Old Indian studies can be at once realized if one turns to the inscriptions of the Achaemenid kings and to the large religious compilation of the Avesta. It was customary in the ninth century A.D. to speak of the language of this book as the *ēvāz ī avastāgh*, 'the language of the Avesta', and we have the same practice in Europe to-day. The Avesta is the oldest repository of the old Iranian religious traditions, modified and adapted by the Zoroastrians. These traditions show many points of contact with the Old Indian traditions of the Vedas. They stand so close indeed that each is illumined by the other. When I add that the languages of the Avesta and the Old Persian inscriptions on the one hand, and the language of the Vedas on the other hand appear as two developments of one language, it will readily be understood that one cannot in the fullest sense read a modern, and therefore comparative, grammar of Old Indian without some knowledge of Old Iranian. By a comparison of the two religious and mythological traditions some knowledge can be gained of an earlier undocumented period. By a comparison of the languages one can reach back to a common linguistic period, and thence proceed from this unity of dialect to a comparison with other Indo-European languages. But if Iranian studies are indispensable to the Indianist, the Iranian scholar finds throughout that he must fill the gaps in his more scanty and badly transmitted material by a full use of the Indian tradition.

After the old period of contact the two traditions rapidly diverged. To so great an extent did this take place that the Indians could eventually refer to the Iranians as breakers of religious laws and *anārya*, that is, non-Aryan.

The classical scholar will probably feel that Persia, even if his bias be to look through Greek eyes upon the barbarians, with a prejudice equally familiar to us in the old Indian books in Indian judgments upon foreigners, was from an early period close to his hand. He will remember that many Greeks were subjects of the Great King. But the Indians were more remote, until at last Alexander the Macedonian broke down this barrier of remoteness. His invasion of North-western India brought the Greek to the influence of India.

The Persian boundaries had long marched with India. In the time of the Achaemenids, Darius claimed the region which he called Hinduš, that is, the Indus land, as a Persian province. It is possible that earlier Kambōjiya, whom the Greeks and Romans called Cambyses, had had a connection with the Kamboja people, whom we know on the borders of India.

It is therefore easy to understand how the historian, looking from the west, has been tempted particularly to essay the task of writing the history of North-western India and of the Greek kingdom of Bactria, which succeeded the eastern excursion of Alexander. It has been a period of great obscurity.

Historical texts with exact chronology are not found in older Indian literature. The precision, which the Chinese scholar, annalist or biographer, gave to his work, and equally the philosophical approach to history of the Greek, are lacking. It has therefore been a slow laborious task to win back from time a small portion of history from incidental allusions, elaborated legends, or from the coins and inscriptions. The period of Hellenistic and Indian intercourse seems to have proved particularly fascinating. It is indeed the honour of Cambridge in the person of my predecessor, Professor Rapson, to have given form to the nebulous north-west from the light of his numismatic learning. But many problems still await solution in this field, and we may expect in the future many a student to be drawn to the work of its interpretation.

We may now look back upon the researches of almost a hundred and fifty years of Indian studies. I have so far touched exceedingly briefly upon the material which has been made known of the literatures and history of the land of India itself. I have referred to the two streams of the tradition, the Indian and the Iranian, arising from a common source.

I have now to speak of the exciting discoveries which began to be made some fifty years ago in Central Asia, from the lands extending from the ancient Sogdiana, with its capital Samarkand, to the confines of China. This new material has been welcomed eagerly by those to whom the reading of a literature inevitably exotic and, for those whose taste has been formed by Greek models, at times somewhat bizarre and formless, was insufficient, to whom the endless disputes on Vedic religion and Vedic interpretations were unsatisfying, and to whom the problems of ancient philosophies were not altogether captivating. It began to be possible to piece together the scattered evidences of the culture of India outside India to the north. For this a new method was necessary. It was necessary to escape from the tyranny of a Sanskrit tradition, confined to works written in Sanskrit, to the freedom of other languages. The most brilliant exponent of this method was M. Sylvain Lévi, whose learning embraced the larger part of the range of literatures of this extra-Indian culture, and in whose footsteps we would gladly follow.

It was a religion, Buddhism, which brought about this wide extension of Indian ideas. Buddhism set itself to win the whole world.

It has been possible to trace the gradual advance of Buddhist schools from Magadha in the east, the home of the religion, to the west and the north-west of India. It was taught by the Mathurā school of the west how the Buddha, the founder, himself had come to the west, and by his prophecies and acts sanctified many sites in that region. There relics of the Buddha were kept in reverent honour.

Beyond Gandhāra, the region of modern Peshawar, in the north-west, the faith in various forms went northwards to Bactria and north-eastwards to Kashmir. Large monastic establishments arose under royal patronage. The Nava Vihāra, the New Monastery, of Bactra or Balkh, became famous. By the third century A.D. Buddhism was flourishing in the lands beyond Sogdiana, in Khotan and the Krorayina kingdom on the northern frontiers of China. The advance was rapid and enthusiastic. The profound and subtle Buddhist teachers of India, Vasubandhu, Asaṅga, Nāgārjuna and their fellow-scholars, became the glory also of these lands. Early the Chinese too entered upon the work of translation. They recorded how at first they studied with the monks of Kuci, and with the monks of Khotan, and how later they visited, through great perils of desert and mountain, the holy land itself and brought back manuscripts, images and relics. Not only, however, did they relish and dispute upon the subtleties of the doctrines of the person of the Buddha, but they loved, as the Buddhist monks had from the first loved, to hear worldly tales with the golden threads of Buddhist morality inwoven. Hundreds of these tales came to the East. They were of every kind, beast fables, tales of popular life, epic narratives, humour, legends both of mythical and of historical persons, as of the kings, the enemies or friends of the faith, of Aśoka, of Kaniṣka and of Caṣṭana.

In Chinese and Tibetan translations this literature has survived in abundance and was added to, so that we have among other new compositions important lexicons in which Sanskrit is explained in Chinese and Tibetan. But the exciting discoveries of the past fifty years have been the recovery of large portions of the lost literatures of the lands, now overrun by Turks, which lay along the routes to China. Sogdian, Khotanese, Kuchean, Agnean, Turkish, Krorayinese and early Chinese and Tibetan literary treasures were added to the existing bulk of Buddhist literature. In the languages of India much of this material had ceased to exist. With the literature of Buddhism were recovered many documents concerned with the history of Central

Asia. It is an acquisition most flatteringly welcome. Chinese sources for the history of this region have been all too scanty. The very names of the kings of Khotan and Agni and Krorayina had been forgotten till the new discoveries restored them to us.

Among the more unexpected of these discoveries was that of the use of a Middle Indian dialect, similar to that used in the north-west of India, written in the Kharoṣṭhī script, as the language of administration in Krorayina. Most of these documents are official, but a few are literary both in Middle Indian and in Sanskrit. Almost eight hundred have been published, and others no doubt exist. It was in Khotan itself that the now famous birch-bark manuscript of the Dharmapada, 'the words of religion', was found. The half we at present possess—we still await the publication of the greater part, which has lain since 1897 in St Petersburg—has revealed the Middle Indian language which has left so great a trace in the languages of Central Asia, particularly in Khotan.

These then are, if I may so style them, the studies of Greater India. They have leapt beyond the barriers of the Sanskrit language. It is no longer a study of books in Sanskrit, but of all documents which in any way help us to elucidate the long, complex and fascinating political and cultural history of Asia. It is a trail which leads from India by the northern route over the Pamirs and by the southern seas as far as Japan. Traces of this Indian influence can even now be seen there in the Sanskrit words, under slight disguises, which are still remembered, as when we see *bikara* for the Sanskrit *vihāra*, that is, a monastery, and *rakan* for the Indian *arahan*, the title of the saintly man. Here too during the past fifty years there has been a great revival of Sanskrit learning in the service of Buddhism, and we now receive from Japan important editions of Sanskrit texts.

Buddhism has thus led the Indianist to the countries of Central Asia and to China and Tibet. Not only however have new avenues in the history of Buddhism been opened, but the history and culture of these lands have themselves become important. Along these routes was brought the silk of China to the west, and the plants of Persia came to China. Here much of

(23)

interest to the general culture of the world remains to be investigated.

The new discoveries have made known lost languages, which had flourished in these countries till, after the tenth century A.D., the Turkish language replaced them.

Of the languages of Kuci and Agni much has been published under the name of Tocharian. No one who has heard of Indo-European languages is ignorant of this discovery. Although we still await the publication of many of the texts, enough has been published to show clearly what type of language they represent. We have in them a new branch of the Indo-European group. It is attested at a regrettably late date, but has much of great importance for general Indo-European studies. It is unfortunate that we have not yet had an English specialist for this study.

Equally unknown were two Iranian languages, the Sogdian and the Khotanese. For this latter I confess to a particular attachment. In Khotanese we have material of great diversity. Translations from Sanskrit are numerous. But there are also documents of great interest concerned with the country itself. Among the most important are the ambassadorial reports, if that is not too grand a title, sent to the Khotanese king. Lighter matters are also represented, as when we find a schoolboy's exercises. He will solemnly copy out the advice: Learn quickly that you may not be punished, and similar wisdom, or will write Sanskrit conversations and add his own rendering. Some of the translations are accompanied also by the original Sanskrit text, which may have perished elsewhere. From this too we learn how they treated Sanskrit in Khotan. At first sight it seemed mere corruption, but it can now be seen to be rather a deliberate modification in accordance with the pronunciation of the language which prevailed among them, and so is legitimate and of interest for Indian studies.

It is natural that a certain amount of reflected light should be thrown also upon the history of India itself. Much has yet to be done before all the historical information is available, but I may mention one discovery of particular interest, which has recently become known to me. Among the celebrated kings of India was Kaniṣka. His date is not yet quite sure, but he may have reigned in the second century A.D. In Chinese texts, where he is often mentioned, a mysterious epithet appears before his name, the epithet *ṣṣan-tan*. Much has been written on this word. But the solution came only with the reading of a Khotanese text. Here at last a legend was found, a legend of Kaniṣka and Aśvaghoṣa, his *kalyāṇamitra* or spiritual friend. The text begins in Sanskrit but soon changes to Khotanese, and corresponding to the unknown Chinese word I found *Candra*: *Candra Kaniṣka*. *Candra* is of course the Indian word for 'moon', and no doubt this discovery will give rise to considerable speculation.

But the Khotanese were not content to be only recipients of Buddhist legends. They developed their own. They declared that the Buddha himself had visited the hill of Gośṛṅga in Khotan, and had there prophesied the future greatness of the faith among the Khotanese. They claimed the particular favour of the Bodhisattva Vairocana. They believed that the founder of the kingdom of Khotan had been a son of Aśoka, the great patron of the faith, born when Aśoka was visiting Khotan. They had in their country most holy places and the names of many of these holy places have reached us in Khotanese and Tibetan books.

It will be understood how delightful it was to find a Buddhist poem, the Jātaka-stava, which had been composed in the Sāmanyā monastery, for this name had long been known in the faithful record of the Chinese pilgrim Hüan-tsang, and more recently in Tibetan books. Among the Khotanese rolls has been found also the legend of Aśoka and his son Kunāla, who was slandered by his stepmother.

All this activity in the service of the Buddha is a testimony to its importance in the life of Khotan. Of the music and dramatic performances of which the Khotanese were so fond, nothing has survived. The name they used for the drama was Indian, the word *nālai*, and it is probable that they knew the Sanskrit drama adapted to Buddhist purposes, known to us now from frag-ments discovered in Central Asia. Of the elaborate festivals we learn from the Chinese travellers. Fa-hien in the fifth century A.D. tells us how on the first day of the fourth month, probably therefore the month they called Bra-khaysdya, they swept and watered and deco-rated the streets of the city. The king, the queen and the court ladies took their places over the city gate. The monks of the Gomati monastery, accounted chief of the fourteen greater monasteries, led the first procession. An image of the Buddha adorned with the seven precious things, and attended with images of Bodhisattvas, was brought on a car to the city. When the images were one hundred paces from the gate, the king came forth barefooted and bearing flowers and incense. He bowed before the images and scattered the flowers. Then as the car entered the city, the ladies from the top of the gate cast down upon it flowers of many kinds. The processions, from each monastery in turn, continued till the fourteenth day of the month. At the end the king and queen returned to the palace.

Of all this splendour of the religion we have only Chinese accounts. But among the newly discovered documents we find a panegyric of King Viṣa Dharma and eulogies of King Viṣa Saṅgrāma. More may yet be found when all the documents have been examined.

I have still to mention Turkish. Turkish has been well represented among the Central Asian manuscripts. Many of the texts are translations from Sanskrit and official documents. For the most part these have been texts written in the Sogdian script, which is of Aramaic origin, but the old Turkish script of the Orqon inscriptions has also been discovered. But for Indian studies a still more interesting fact is the use of the Indian Brāhmī script for the writing of Turkish. Only a small part has yet been published, but that little is of importance. It is one of the difficulties of Turkish studies that the scripts usually employed do not clearly distinguish the vowels. This the Indian alphabet was able to do. We can therefore see how these Turks understood their own language. It has not been usual to associate Turks with Sanskrit studies. It is therefore interesting that one of these texts is bilingual. A Sanskrit text is explained in Turkish.

The Khotanese texts are likely to be of importance for Turkish history. Here there are many references to the Turkish chiefs, to the Khaghan, the khans, the tegins, the chors, and the saghuns; and reference also to the many Turkish tribes. Chinese histories of this period have little to say of the Turks in the tenth century, and the new information is therefore doubly welcome.

One division of Indian literature which deserves a special mention is the medical. This literature was assiduously cultivated by the Buddhists, and the earliest extant medical manuscript in Sanskrit was brought from Central Asia. Translations of medical texts were made into a variety of Asiatic languages. We have more or less fragmentary texts in Turkish, Kuchean, Agnean and Khotanese. Among the Khotanese is a manuscript containing a medical text in the original Sanskrit together with the Khotanese rendering, beside others preserved only in translation.

I have said before that the Buddhists have ever loved the telling of tales. They brought a vast number with them from India, and of these versions have turned up among the Central Asian rolls. It was natural to find the more famous Buddhist tales, as those of Aśoka or of Sudhana, who with many labours sought his lost fairy wife over the mountains. But it was not expected that the great Brahmanical hero, Rāma, should appear here also in a Buddhist environment. Yet this has happened. We have now Central Asian and Tibetan variants of the legend to set beside the Indian and the Javanese.

For Iranian the linguistic importance of these discoveries has been especially great. Among them are the oldest extant manuscripts of Iranian languages. The Khotanese is particularly useful, for here we find a complete description of an Iranian language, with a full contemporary notation of all the sounds, both vowels and consonants. This we find nowhere else in Iranian studies. Owing to the imperfect system of notation adopted by the Semites and those who received their alphabets from them, including ourselves, it is rare to find a completely recorded language.

Nor should I omit to mention that the historical geographer will have many new names to add to his maps when all these new materials are available. For these Central Asian countries there has existed hitherto scanty information in Ptolemy's Geography and, also, more copiously, in Chinese books. But in these new sources we have the uncorrupted native form.

I turn now to another aspect of Indian studies, which equally transcends the purely Indian interest. This is the linguistic aspect, the importance of Sanskrit for Indo-European studies. Sanskrit grammarians had carried very far the analysis of their own language and had forged a complex technical vocabulary. The recognition in Europe of a connection, which may be called a sisterly connection, of Sanskrit with other Asiatic languages such as Persian and Armenian, and with European languages, such as English, Greek, Latin, Irish, Russian, Lithuanian and Albanian, led to the development of a discipline which we know in Cambridge as Comparative Philology. We have now a Chair in this subject and I need here only indicate the position of Indian and Iranian in this study.

The problem of the relationship existing between the members of this group of languages, the Indo-European, as we call them for want of a better name, has produced an enormous literature. This has been constantly overhauled and modified as new facts have been recognized. A revolution is proceeding at the present time, which, if it should establish itself, will make all books before 1935 obsolete.

In this study Old Indian and Iranian have had an honourable place. The oldest Indian texts are of uncertain date, but may be, as I have said above, in parts, of about 1200 B.C. Dated texts of an earlier period are therefore found in the Kassite vocabulary and the Hittite documents from Asia Minor. But even beside these the Indian texts hold an important position yielding little in date. With Hittite and Greek, Indian represents for us the oldest extant form of the Indo-European language.

The exaggerated importance which was attached to Sanskrit in the early days of comparative grammar has long since been rectified for the initiate, although it may be seen still lingering among the uninitiated. But it is still indispensable to Indo-European studies. Indian and Iranian together have given valuable assistance in the determination of the consonantal correspondence in the original system. In regard to the vocalic system their importance is much less.

Linguistic method applied to any group of languages has proceeded from the study of Indo-European. It is here that the method has been elaborated. Sanskrit therefore has a claim in all linguistic work. It has worthily been admitted to a place in Classical studies.

What of the future of these studies? What has been done and what remains to do? If we envisage a time when all Indian and Iranian knowledge will be recorded in encyclopaedias, that time is far off. Indeed much of the attraction of these studies lies in the newness and the pioneer work which has still to be done. But in more than a hundred years of Indian work, much has been accomplished. All the important Vedic texts are available in critical editions. We have copious works of reference for the Vedas, dictionaries, concordance, realia, grammars and commentaries. But an up-to-date dictionary for the whole of Sanskrit literature does not yet exist. For the later classical Sanskrit and for the Middle Indian dialects we are less well off. Often critical editions have not even been attempted. The very abundance of manuscript material often puts the task beyond the powers of one man for even a single text. An admirable edition of the huge epic, the Mahābhārata, has been begun by a committee. We have a few good editions of dramas. For the Jaina and Buddhist books only a beginning has been made. Critical editions have been more particularly difficult for the

Buddhist works, since they are preserved in many languages.

Excellent studies have been published on all branches of Indian learning and the subjects treated are many: religion, philosophy, logic, astronomy, astrology, medicine, poetry, fiction, law, grammar, ethnology, economics. But in each branch much remains for the future.

I must here bring this lecture to its close.

For the greatness of the subject the number of serious students has always been small in England. We should ascribe this to the regrettable fact that it has remained an unremunerative study. In this it suffers with all Oriental studies. But one cannot view without concern the somewhat haphazard way in which the present disregard for the training of good students, future professors, is operating in England.

I should wish however to end on a higher note. I can gladly commend Indian and Iranian studies alike as offering a wide field for new discoveries and, for the less adventurous mind, a rich and varied literature of intense human interest.